CALM
MINDFULNESS FOR KIDS

Written by **Wynne Kinder M. Ed.**

Contents

DK | Penguin Random House

Author Wynne Kinder M. Ed.
Consultant Dr Lana Jackson

Project Editor Olivia Stanford
Senior Art Editor Fiona Macdonald
Designer Bettina Myklebust Stovne
Design Assistant Xiao Lin
Jacket Co-ordinator Francesca Young
Jacket Designer Fiona Macdonald
Producers, Pre-Production Nadine King, Sophie Chatellier
Senior Producer Isabell Schart
Managing Editor Laura Gilbert
Managing Art Editor Diane Peyton Jones

Photographer Ruth Jenkinson
Photographic Assistant Elena Lopez-Fortin
Illustrations Bettina Myklebust Stovne, Xiao Lin
DTP Designer Nityanand Kumar
Creative Director Helen Senior
Publishing Director Sarah Larter

First published in Great Britain in 2019 by
Dorling Kindersley Limited
80 Strand, London, WC2R 0RL

A CIP catalogue record for this book is available from the British Library.
ISBN: 978-0-2413-4229-9

Printed and bound in China

A WORLD OF IDEAS:
SEE ALL THERE IS TO KNOW

www.dk.com

Safety information

Please supervise and help your child as necessary. Be aware of your child's limitations and encourage them not to force or strain themselves. Awareness and attention practices might be mentally challenging, and any physical activity has some risk of injury. While the exercises may be helpful, they are not a substitute for medical advice or intervention if your child suffers from any medical condition.

Introduction

Hey there! Welcome to *Calm*. You are probably wondering where this book came from and how mindfulness for kids really works. Well, here's the story.

I am a teacher and a parent, and way back in time I was a kid, just like you. My many years have been filled with both challenging and easy moments, like yours. The rough days seemed stressful, full of busy schedules, worries about school, heavy emotions, and fights with my brother. Everyone has things to get through and learn from – those were some of mine.

I found mindfulness as a grown-up, when I was teaching. I wish I knew about it when I was younger. It would have been great to have safe, helpful tools that I could explore, learn, and practise on my own – personal tools that would help me manage my emotions, understand my thoughts, and feel good in my body.

I tried all kinds of mindful exercises for myself – quiet, active, noisy, still, and even a few that seemed a little weird. Then I learned to share them with my students and with my own kids. This book is a collection of mindful practices that you can try, either on your own, or with family and friends.

Here's a strategy that has worked for many of my students when they got started – try each mindful practice on like shoes. Keep in mind that some will fit you, some won't. Some might fit later, and some may never quite work for you. No worries – they are yours to explore, adjust, repeat, or put away for later.

Enjoy,

Wynne

Wynne Kinder has been teaching for almost 30 years. She started with maths, science, reading, and writing, and in 2004, moved onto mindfulness. Wynne continues to explore mindfulness and works with teachers and families. She has created training and curriculums for teachers and co-authored online resources for GoNoodle.

Our minds can easily be filled with busy thoughts. Even if they are pleasant, too many things going on in your head can be distracting, or feel overwhelming.

Mindfulness

Mindfulness is a big word for a simple idea – it is paying attention, with care, to one moment at a time. People are often distracted. It takes practice to use your senses to focus on one thing and learn to live in the present.

You can practise being mindful by focusing your attention on one thing at a time: what you see, hear, smell, taste, or feel.

FOR THE GROWN-UPS...

Learning mindfulness can be tricky at first. Adults can find information in these circles on how to encourage and share the experience, as well as when the exercises can help your child.

We often think about conversations with friends and replying to messages.

Perhaps you have music practice to do and are thinking about when to do it.

Maybe you're worried about how well you've done on a recent test.

You might be distracted by thinking about a new toy you want to play with.

In mindfulness, you put your thoughts gently to one side and focus your mind on what is happening right now.

How to enjoy this book

There are six chapters in this book, such as Focus and Calm, so you can choose what you need, when you need it. In each chapter you will find a mix of mindful exercises and crafts to explore, either alone or with a friend.

Introductions to each chapter explain what the exercises will help with.

Mindful exercises show you what to do.

Step-by-step activities have lists of what you need as well as how to do them.

Picture pages will help get you thinking mindfully.

With practice, your attention can get **stronger**.

Your **attention** can focus, shift, zoom, settle, expand, and wander.

Focus

Your brain has many important jobs to do. It allows you to smell, taste, and see, all automatically. The attention part of your mind keeps you aware of what is happening inside you and around you. In mindfulness, you try to focus your attention on one thing at a time.

Everyone's attention will **drift** or get **distracted** and that's okay.

Clap focus

You can get to know what your attention can do by focusing it on something. Creating sensations can give you something to focus on.

1 **Try to focus your attention** on how your hands feel. Now clap them three times, then stop.

2 **What sensations can you feel?** See if you can zoom your focus in on one part, such as the tip of your right little finger.

Clapping will create a sensation in your hands.

Try expanding your attention to your whole hand, and then to just one part of it.

9

1

Focus your eyes and your attention on one object in the room. Maybe point to it with your finger as your eyes look there.

2

Now, move your attention to another object, this time without pointing. If you start thinking about something else, bring your focus back to the object.

3

Let your attention be like a spotlight. Look around and rest your attention on each object you find. Try it out on several items in the room.

Pick one object and focus on it – notice its colour and shape.

You might notice as you pay attention to each item that everything else goes out of focus.

Your **attention** can move, wander...

Spend about
10 seconds resting
your attention on
each item.

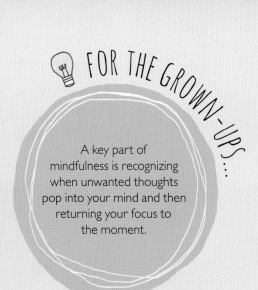

A key part of
mindfulness is recognizing
when unwanted thoughts
pop into your mind and then
returning your focus to
the moment.

Spotlight focus

Mindfulness is about attention. Sometimes
our minds drift and we think about all sorts
of things at once. With practice, we can
notice what our attention does and move it
by choice, like a spotlight.

Try not to be
distracted by
what you plan to
do later. Keep your
attention on now.

After you've
focused on
the last object,
close your
eyes for a
few breaths.

... return, and rest in one place.

You can close your eyes or look away – no peeking in the bag!

You can challenge your partner to find a particular object in the bag.

Feel with your *fingers*, but be aware with your *mind*.

Pick an object and feel its shape, weight, and texture. Try describing it before guessing what it is.

You can play this game with your child. To make it more challenging, choose objects that are quite similar, such as five keys, and ask your child to feel for the differences.

FOR THE GROWN-UPS...

Make sure you don't put anything sharp into the bag!

What's in the bag?

Our senses give us lots of information about the world around us. We usually pay attention by looking, but you can play a game that helps you focus with your other senses.

Mystery object

Fill a bag with a few objects. Make sure they all have different textures – for example, smooth, rough, soft, or fluffy. Then ask a friend to put a hand in the bag and see if they can guess what's inside. Take turns filling the bag and using your sense of touch to guess!

What you'll need:

- Small bag, container, or pillowcase
- A selection of objects with different textures
- A friend

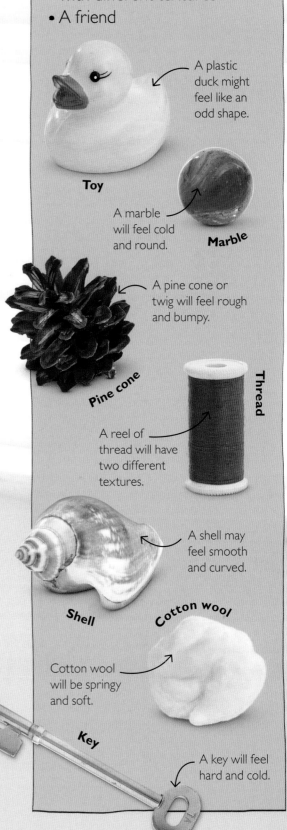

A plastic duck might feel like an odd shape.

Toy

A marble will feel cold and round.

Marble

A pine cone or twig will feel rough and bumpy.

Pine cone

A reel of thread will have two different textures.

Thread

A shell may feel smooth and curved.

Shell

Cotton wool

Cotton wool will be springy and soft.

A key will feel hard and cold.

Key

1 First, **stamp your feet** for the time it takes to breathe in and out once. Then pause and notice the sensation of your feet on the floor.

Tilt from side to side just enough to create a feeling where your body meets the chair.

Feet, seat, and hands practice

In this mindful practice, you will learn to move your attention to different parts of your body by creating sensations to focus your thoughts on.

2 Next, **gently lean your upper body** from side to side three times. Then sit still. Can you feel where you are sitting on the chair?

FOR THE GROWN-UPS...

After practising together, ask your child which was the easiest spot to move their attention to. The feet, seat, or hands? Ask why they think this is.

Your hands might feel warm after you have rubbed them together.

3 **Finally, rub your hands together** for the count of 10. Then stop and place your hands on your lap. Focus on the feelings in your hands. Notice how you moved your attention throughout your body!

Notice how you can **move** your **focus** to different parts of your body.

15

My body breathes

Your body breathes all of the time, so breathing is always with you. Checking in on breathing helps your mind focus on the present moment – on what's happening right now.

Breathe normally and concentrate on the movement of your ribs as you breathe.

Put your fingers on the front of your ribs and your thumbs on your back.

Can you feel your ribcage pushing your fingers and thumbs apart as you breathe in?

Expanding ribs

Try resting your hands on each side of your ribcage. Notice which way your ribs move when you breathe in, or inhale, and when you breathe out, or exhale.

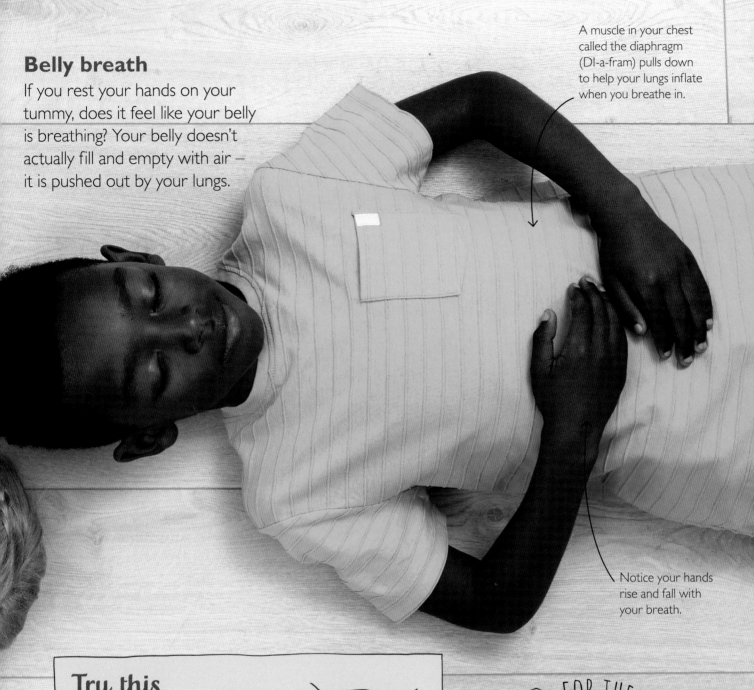

Belly breath

If you rest your hands on your tummy, does it feel like your belly is breathing? Your belly doesn't actually fill and empty with air – it is pushed out by your lungs.

A muscle in your chest called the diaphragm (DI-a-fram) pulls down to help your lungs inflate when you breathe in.

Notice your hands rise and fall with your breath.

Try this

With your hands on your stomach, breathe in, letting your hands lift off your tummy, as if they are on the surface of a balloon that is being blown up. As you breathe out, let your hands return to your stomach, as if the balloon is deflating.

FOR THE GROWN-UPS

Concentrating on breathing is a great way to focus on the present. We usually don't notice our breath, but it is always there to come back to.

17

Take a walk

Busy days can leave us feeling tired and stressed. When you want to slow down and unplug, practise focusing on the world around you. If you can, go for a walk in nature and use your senses to take it in.

Use your eyes to notice everything around you. Look at all the different shapes, colours, and sizes of everything you see.

Spending time in a forest, or "forest bathing", can help you feel calm. All you have to do is be there and enjoy the green surroundings.

What can you hear? Birds singing? Aeroplanes overhead? Some sounds might be up-close and others in the distance. Pause and listen closely for hard-to-hear sounds.

Your sense of touch makes you aware of temperature and texture. Try holding a twig – how does it feel? Is it heavy or light?

Smells can be challenging to detect. Be still and close your eyes – let your nose do its job. What can you smell?

Focusing your attention can be a tool for **calming** your mind.

With practice, **mindfully** moving your body can help calm you.

Calm

Being calm means feeling settled and quiet. It's easy when you are tired, but not when you are full of energy. When your energy doesn't match what you need – for example, if you're wide awake at bedtime – mindful exercises can be useful ways to lower your energy and calm down.

Your in-breath **increases** energy, while your out-breath **calms**.

High-five breath

This is a handy practice to help you feel calm by paying attention to your breath. Matching mindful movement with your breathing can be calming. Take your time.

FOR THE GROWN-UPS...

Briefly pausing at the top and bottom of each breath is healthy, but holding your breath can cause tension or anxious feelings.

1

Starting at the outside edge of your thumb, breathe in and use your index finger to trace up to the top. When you breathe out, slowly trace down the other side.

2

Keep breathing in and out, tracing up and down for a total of five breaths until you reach the other side of your hand.

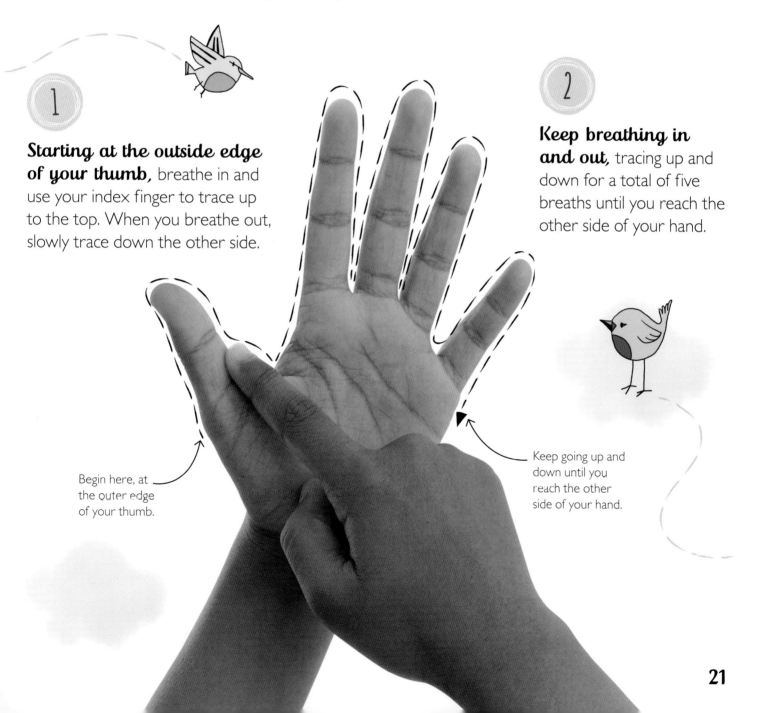

Begin here, at the outer edge of your thumb.

Keep going up and down until you reach the other side of your hand.

Glitter jar

Sometimes our thoughts and emotions can get stirred up and this makes it hard to think clearly. A glitter jar can be a tool to help you to settle your feelings.

What you'll need:

• Water
• An empty jar with a lid
• Clear PVA glue
• Glitter (different sizes work best)

1 **Pour water into the jar,** then add a big squeeze of glue. This will make your glitter swirl around and settle slowly.

The glue and water will mix when you shake it later.

2 **Add glitter to the jar.** It might float at first, but don't worry. Different colours can represent different emotions.

Feel your **thoughts** *and* **emotions** *settling with the glitter.*

The glitter will mix together as it swirls around.

☆ FOR THE GROWN-UPS...

When you want to dispose of the jar, it is best to strain the glitter out using kitchen paper and to put it in the bin. Most glitter is made of plastic and can enter waterways if put down the sink.

3 **Put the lid on tightly** and gently shake your jar. Watch the glitter get stirred up.

4

Watch the glitter as it falls. How many out-breaths does it take for the glitter to settle completely?

5

Anytime you feel stirred up inside, shake the jar and patiently watch the glitter fall. How do you feel as the glitter settles?

23

1

Sit tall, like a building. Stack your hands in front of you — the one below is the ground floor and the other is a lift that can go up and down.

Place your palms together with your hands flat.

Your hand might only reach shoulder height as you breathe in, or it might go above your head.

2

As you breathe in, raise the top hand up. Keep moving it until you finish breathing in.

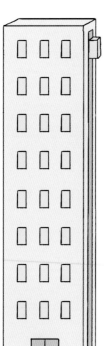

Lift breath

This exercise matches your breathing with movement. You can use it as a tool to help you pause and calm down.

Try this

Try one or two breaths with your eyes closed. See if you can predict when your top hand will meet your bottom hand — this might take practice.

3

As you breathe out, bring the lift down again. Try to get your hands to meet just as you run out of air.

Bring the lift down steadily with your out-breath.

Your bottom hand stays in the same place as the top hand moves.

FOR THE GROWN-UPS...

When practised regularly, this exercise can be useful when your child is feeling anxious or stressed.

25

Power on, power off

Sometimes we can feel like we are too full of energy. You can practise controlling different muscles to manage your own energy, by turning them on and off.

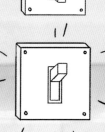

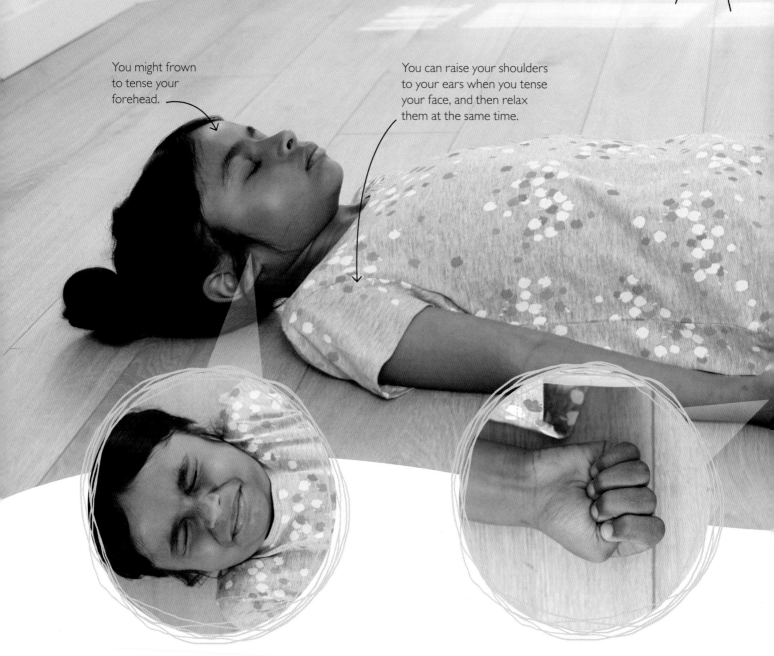

You might frown to tense your forehead.

You can raise your shoulders to your ears when you tense your face, and then relax them at the same time.

 1 **As you breathe in,** turn the power on in your face. Tighten all the muscles you can. When you breathe out, turn the power off and relax your face.

 2 **Ball your hands into fists.** Your arms might tense, too – that's all right. Breathe in with fists, then breathe out and release them.

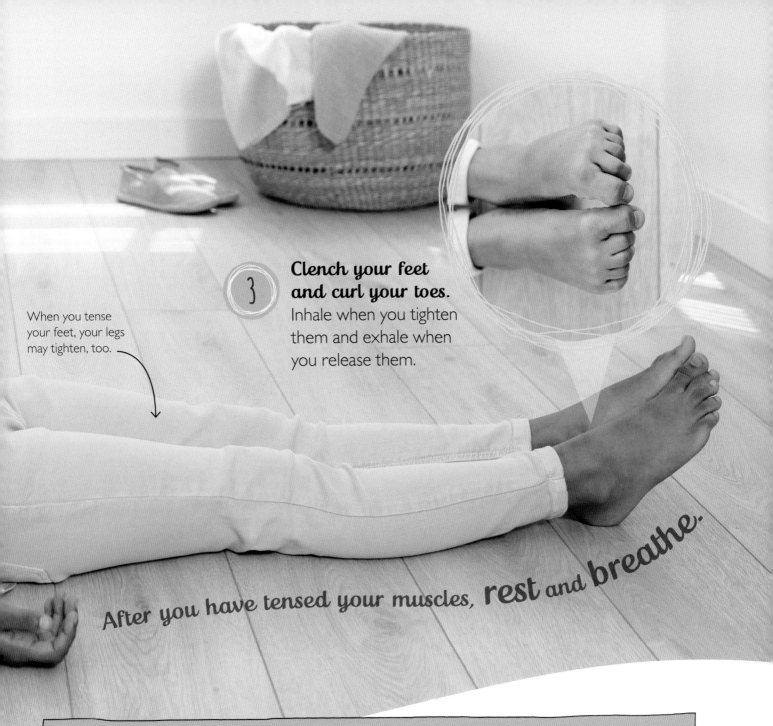

When you tense your feet, your legs may tighten, too.

3 **Clench your feet and curl your toes.** Inhale when you tighten them and exhale when you release them.

*After you have tensed your muscles, **rest** and **breathe.***

Try this

Lie down somewhere comfortable and try turning all your power on at the same time. Remember to tense when you inhale and then relax when you exhale. Afterwards, go ahead and rest.

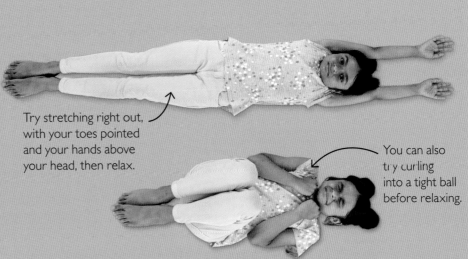

Try stretching right out, with your toes pointed and your hands above your head, then relax.

You can also try curling into a tight ball before relaxing.

Waves of breath

Notice how your breath moves in and out like waves on the shore. Your breath is always with you and it is a great place to rest your attention to help you feel calm.

Try imagining your breath moving like smooth waves rolling in and out at the beach. Keep the picture of the ocean in your mind and watch the waves come in and go out.

Match each breath you take with the waves in your mind. As you breathe in, imagine the waves washing in, and as you breathe out, watch them retreat.

When you breathe normally, you only inhale or exhale about 10 per cent of the space in your lungs. This increases when you exercise or take a big breath.

Try taking one bigger-than-usual breath with the next wave coming in. Imagine this wave going further out than the smaller waves before it.

Reaching, stretching, and bending are **big** ways to move.

Move

Mindfulness involves noticing your feelings, thoughts, and sensations. It can be easier to notice things when you move. Moving mindfully is all about listening to your body and paying attention, even when you are doing things you wouldn't normally think about – like walking.

Circling, twisting, and rotating help us **loosen** our bodies.

Our bodies are amazing tools for strength and **movement.**

From the **top**

Notice what you feel in your head, neck, and shoulders. Start this exercise with small movements, so you can pay close attention and pause, adjust, or do less, depending on what you feel.

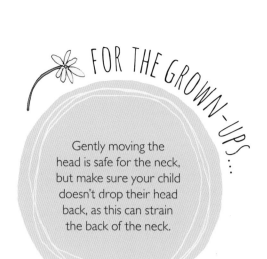

FOR THE GROWN-UPS...

Gently moving the head is safe for the neck, but make sure your child doesn't drop their head back, as this can strain the back of the neck.

1

Stand tall and relaxed.
Carefully lift and lower your chin a few times, as slowly as you wish. Don't tip your head back, though.

2

With your chin level, turn to look left. Pause, then return to the centre. Now turn to the right and then back to the centre.

3

Breathe out and tilt your head to the left. Then breathe in, up to the centre. Try this on both sides.

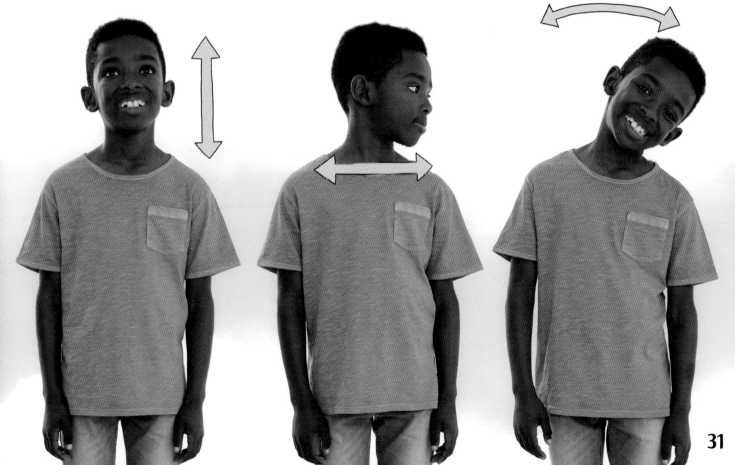

Rainbow breath

Matching your movement to your breath can either give you more energy or steady your mind and body. This exercise requires a little space around you and a little imagination inside you.

Stand tall and still. Let your shoulders relax and your arms hang by your sides.

Relax your hands with your palms forwards.

Finish with your arms shoulder-width apart.

Breathe in as you raise your arms wide. Then reach high and let your palms turn to face each other.

Try this

You can draw an even bigger rainbow by starting with your hands by your knees.

Fold forwards and drop your arms down to wherever is comfortable.

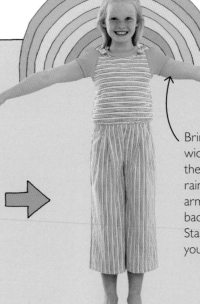

Bring your arms wide and up, then draw a giant rainbow as your arms come down, back to your knees. Stand up tall when you're done.

As you bring your arms down, let your palms turn to face forwards again.

3

Let your hands float down as you breathe out. Keep your arms straight and imagine you are drawing a rainbow above you.

Some children might be able to imagine a rainbow more easily with their eyes closed. You can help them to visualize a rainbow by naming the colours they would see.

FOR THE GROWN-UPS...

1

Breathe in as you press your hands forwards with your palms flat. Pause to notice unwanted emotions, then breathe out to let them go and smoothly drop your arms to your sides.

Press forwards like there is an invisible wall in front of you.

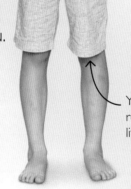

Your elbows can be straight or slightly bent.

2

Repeat the exercise, but this time imagine you are pressing against two walls either side of you.

Your knees can remain soft with a little bend in them.

Press and let go

We can all hang onto emotions, even after we are done with them. Your body can help you practise letting them go.

3

The third time you repeat the exercise, reach and press up, as if you are pushing against an invisible ceiling. Then float your arms down.

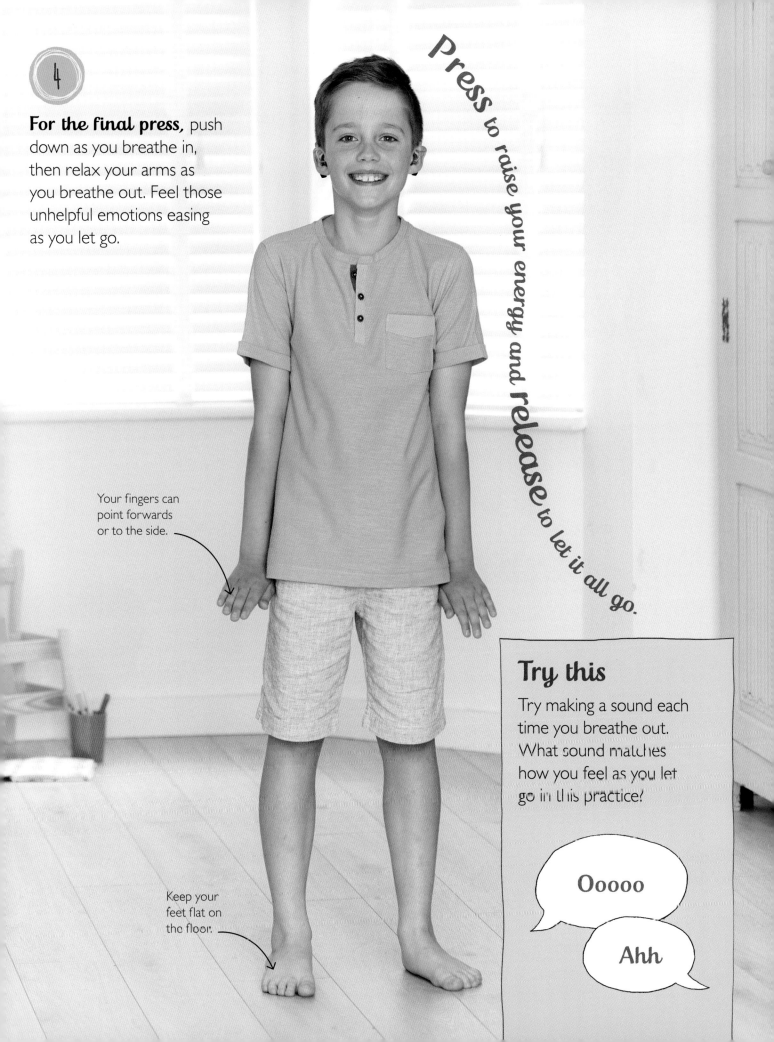

4

For the final press, push down as you breathe in, then relax your arms as you breathe out. Feel those unhelpful emotions easing as you let go.

Press to raise your energy and release to let it all go.

Your fingers can point forwards or to the side.

Keep your feet flat on the floor.

Try this

Try making a sound each time you breathe out. What sound matches how you feel as you let go in this practice?

Ooooo

Ahh

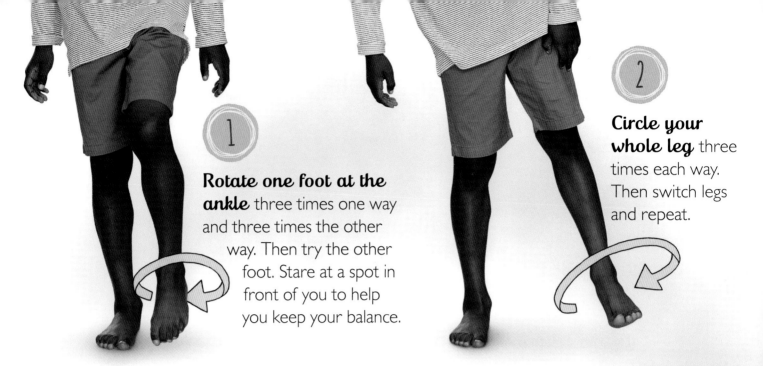

1

Rotate one foot at the ankle three times one way and three times the other way. Then try the other foot. Stare at a spot in front of you to help you keep your balance.

2

Circle your whole leg three times each way. Then switch legs and repeat.

Unwind stress

Stress is the unpleasant feeling we get when we are worried for a long time, and it can make you tense. Moving your body to unwind might help you feel better. It'll be fun to try.

3

Reach your arm out to the side. Slowly rotate it at the shoulder three times each way. Then try your other arm.

4

Keeping your hand relaxed, rotate it at the wrist. You choose the speed. Try one at a time or both together.

FOR THE GROWN-UPS...

Why not try joining in? Unwind together. Add some music or create a song to make it fun.

If your attention wanders, just return it to your body.

Your body might feel tired or tight in some spots. Keep noticing what you feel and only do as much unwinding as feels comfortable.

5

Unwind at your hips by moving them in a circle. Repeat a few times in one direction, then go the other way.

Try this

Explore circling your ribcage — gently go around two times in each direction. Keep your hips and shoulders still while your upper body moves — this can be tricky!

What you'll need:

- Cornflour
- A bowl
- Water
- A spoon
- Food colouring (optional)

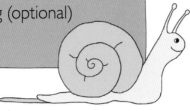

Energy slime

This slime reacts to energy just like people do. You can squeeze it with high energy and release it with low energy. Notice how you feel before and after you make and play with it.

1 **Put a few big scoops of cornflour** in a mixing bowl. You don't have to be exact – about a cupful works well.

2 **Mix in enough water** to make a thick liquid. Go slowly, as it will change thickness very quickly. If you add too much, just add some more cornflour.

FOR THE GROWN-UPS...

When your child is done with their slime, let it dry out overnight, then throw it in the bin. You can wash it away, but use plenty of water so it doesn't block the sink.

3 **Add a few drops of food colouring** if you wish. Carefully stir to mix it in.

When you squeeze it, you will notice that your slime becomes a solid!

Watch out – food colouring can stain.

When released, the slime will melt. Notice the sensations of the slime changing in your hands.

(4)

Try squeezing your slime.
Notice how the slime reacts. When you squeeze it with energy, it becomes solid. When you release the energy, it softens again. Can mindful movement practices help you do the same?

Exhale *while* **releasing** *your slime.*

39

Mindful walking

Walking might be one of the things you do most without thinking. You don't have to concentrate on taking every step. It is a way of getting around, but what if it can be more than that?

To walk mindfully, find a clear bit of floor or a quiet pavement and slow right down. Really be aware of each step. Pay attention to how your weight shifts from one foot to the other.

Think about when you can try this mindful walking practice. In the living room after school? Or before you go to sleep?

Make sure you're in a safe space when you try mindful walking, as you will be concentrating on your steps. If you're outside, make sure you have someone with you.

With each step, breathe in as you lift your foot and breathe out as you set it down again. Focus your eyes on a spot in front of you to stay steady and keep your balance.

To help you focus your attention, think "Breathe in for up and breathe out for down".

41

Life is full of **changes** - they come in all sizes.

Change can be challenging, **exciting,** and fun.

Change

Change might seem scary, but you can learn how to feel better about it. Whether you're moving schools or getting a new sibling, you can practise mindful activities that could help you feel more prepared for new things.

Change is something you can learn to handle, **skilfully.**

STOP practice

Life can feel like it is moving really quickly and you might feel out of control. You can prepare for those times by trying STOP practice. This lets you take a moment for yourself when you need it.

 **1** **S**top moving. Be still right where you are, as long as it is safe to do so.

 2 **T**ake a breath. Focus on your natural breathing, in and out. You don't have to take a big breath.

 **3** **O**bserve. Notice what's going on both on the inside and around you. What does your body feel? What do you see?

 4 **P**roceed. Carry on as you were, or change your approach if you feel you want to.

FOR THE GROWN-UPS...

Encourage a daily STOP practice for you and your child. This can be a helpful tool to make your child mindfully aware of their current state and if a change is needed.

Breathing buddy

You might find that you breathe faster when you are worried about a change. Why not make a breathing buddy, to help you take a few big breaths and restore calm?

 Ask an adult to cut a hole in the bottom of the cup using scissors.

The hole will let you exhale through the cup.

 2 **Decorate your cup** with eyes, ears, a nose, or tail – you can make whatever animal you like, so get creative.

FOR THE GROWN-UPS...

Overbreathing, or hyperventilating, is unusually fast breathing. A few long out-breaths followed by a break (natural breaths) can prevent it.

 3 **Cut some strips of tissue paper** and stick them around the inside edge of the cup with glue or tape. Let the glue dry.

The strips can be attached inside either end of the cup.

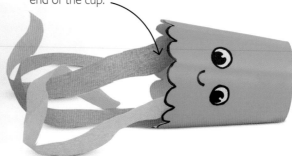

4 **Inhale through your nose** and exhale by blowing through the cup slowly. Try this for three breaths. Then pause. How do you feel on the inside?

Watch your breath moving the streamers.

Try this

You can decorate your breathing buddy to look like any animal you want. Here are some examples to try.

Yawn to reset

At times, we can all feel down. Maybe our emotions are stuck on sad, nervous, disappointed, or mad. It can be hard to figure out what we need. A yawn to reset might help.

Big breath
If you think about it, you might be able to create a yawn. Try standing up, making fists, and stretching your arms up. Breathe in and out through your mouth.

You might stretch up, forwards, or to the side. You get to choose.

FOR THE GROWN-UPS...

Scientists aren't exactly sure why we yawn. It may help us stay alert or even cool our brains. We may yawn when we are tired, and also when we are nervous.

Don't worry if a yawn doesn't come – you're just practising.

When you yawn, notice how your ears, jaw, and throat seem to stretch.

When you yawn, see if people around you yawn, too.

After your yawn, gently relax your arms down and take a moment to notice how you are feeling. Do you feel the same or different inside? There is no right or wrong way to feel.

Reach wide

You can also try spreading your fingers and hands, and doing a big stretch. Reach your arms wide. Your eyes might close as you open your mouth to breathe in.

Plant a seed

Just as seeds change, so do we. Plants grow in different ways, at different speeds, and may need patience – and so do we. Help a seed grow with your care, support, and patience.

Water the seed until the soil is damp, but don't turn it into mud!

Water the seed and then place the pot somewhere sunny.

③

Make a hole with your finger – don't forget to wash your hands afterwards.

Fill your pot with soil and make a hole in it with your finger. Drop in a seed and cover it with enough soil that you can't see it anymore.

②

The dish will stop water leaking out when you water your plant.

What you'll need:

- A plant pot (with holes for water to drain away)
- A dish with sides
- Pebbles
- Soil
- Sunflower seeds
- Water

Put the pot in the dish and add a few pebbles to cover the holes. These will stop the soil from falling out.

Water the pot when it gets dry and practise patience – the seed will take several days to sprout.

FOR THE GROWN-UPS

Planting a few seeds will ensure success, as some may not germinate. Once sprouted, too much sun might wilt the seedling, so adjust its location if needed.

4 **Check your seedling** every day. This is a great time to practise mindfulness for a few minutes. Try to notice any small changes each time you observe it. Eventually, you might need to put it in a bigger pot!

Using your attention, try tracing the path of the river in this picture. Take your time and follow all the twists and turns. Just go with the flow.

Go with the flow

Going with the flow means accepting a situation as it is, and not trying to change it right away. It can be a helpful skill in dealing with unexpected events or surprises.

Imagine yourself as the water in a wiggly river. Notice how it has to take a different path at times, just like we sometimes need to do.

Try drawing a maze with lots of turns and dead ends. Trace the route with your finger. Be patient as you go. Sometimes you can make choices, just like in life.

Occasionally, things will get in your way. Instead of getting stuck or annoyed, pause and look for little changes in what you can do. Go with the flow.

To care means to feel **kindness** and concern for yourself and others.

Care

You have a lot of love and care inside you. Sharing those warm feelings with others can help you feel good, too. Begin with the way you treat yourself. Build on that and you will have more care to give to the world.

Remember to look after **yourself** as well as others.

Caring grows with awareness, attention, and patience.

Open and hug practice

Let your body help you feel love and care. Try giving yourself a hug as a reminder to care for yourself.

FOR THE GROWN-UPS...

Guide your child to think about all the people who care for them as they open their arms, and to embrace that caring feeling with the gentle hug.

1

Sit tall and spread your arms wide. Look up a little and breathe in.

2

Breathe out and wrap your arms around yourself for a hug. Tuck your chin in as you look down. Close your eyes if you wish.

My dog

Who do you care about?
List all the people you care about.
This might include your parents,
grandparents, siblings, and friends.
Think about who looks after you.

I care about my mum.

Caring scrapbook

What you care about affects how you feel and what you do. Think about all the people and things you care for in your life. Maybe make a scrapbook to collect your ideas.

Look after yourself.
Make sure to care for
yourself as well as those
around you. This can be
as simple as keeping clean
and brushing your teeth,
or creating time to try
mindful exercises.

I will read my favourite book before bed.

Remember to
be kind to
yourself
as well as others.

My family

54

My bike

My colourful pens

My sunflower

What would you take with you if you were going on a trip? Why not try listing 10 things you care about? Try to think why each item means a lot to you.

Aim to be kind to everyone around you. It won't just make them feel good, it will make you feel good, too! Think of ways you can do something kind each day.

- Hug someone in your family
- Make a drawing for a friend
- Volunteer to help
- Listen carefully to others
- Share your toys
- Smile

To my best friend:

Mindful eating

We usually eat quickly, barely stopping to really notice what we are eating. What are we missing? Try eating mindfully – being patient and using all your senses to experience your food.

 FOR THE GROWN-UPS...

Encourage your child to try mindful eating one mealtime. You could try eating in silence for five minutes. Notice what feels different about mindful eating and discuss it together.

1

Find a small snack.
A piece of dried fruit works well. First look at it very carefully. Notice its colour, shape, and texture.

2

Let your fingers
sense the temperature and feel of the food. Gently squeeze it – is it squishy? Sticky?

3

Hold it up to your ear and roll it between your finger and thumb. Can you hear anything?

4

Next, raise it to your nose. Take time to smell it. Does it smell familiar? Is your mouth watering?

5

With just the tip of your tongue, taste it. Then place it in your mouth, but count to 10 before you chew. What do you notice? What can you taste?

Try this

See if you can chew one bite of food 15 times. How does it change what you notice about that food? Does the flavour stay the same?

What you'll need:

- Different-coloured pipe cleaners
- Beads to decorate (optional)
- A jar or container
- Water
- Washing-up liquid
- Glycerine

Bubbles of kindness

Sometimes it's hard to share your thoughts and feelings, even nice ones. Why not send out your kind thoughts in bubbles?

Make sure the hole isn't too big or too small.

Make the loop as close to the centre as you can.

Twisting together the two ends will make a handle.

1

Twist together two pipe cleaners to make one thicker one. Then make a loop in the middle and twist together the two ends to make your bubble wand handle.

2

Mix together equal parts of water and washing-up liquid in the jar, then add a splash of glycerine to make your bubble mix.

Try this

You can decorate your bubble wand in different ways. Why not try different shapes, or adding beads to the handle? Beads can help make the handle stronger.

3 **Dip the wand in the bubble mixture** and gently blow a bubble. Imagine your kind thoughts for others filling the bubbles as you watch them float into the world.

Watch out for drips! Bubble mixture can be slippery on the floor. It's best to do this outside.

Ask your child to think about sending kind thoughts not just to friends, but to people they don't get on with. This may encourage a sense of empathy.

☆ FOR THE GROWN-UPS...

Reflect

Wisdom is using the things you have learned to make good decisions. You might get wisdom from stories and books, or from your family and friends. You can also gain wisdom by reflecting, or thinking carefully, about the experiences you've had.

Heart and belly breath

Make a habit of pausing to become more aware of you. Mindfulness reminds you to think about, and connect with, yourself.

☆ FOR THE GROWN-UPS...

You can help your child to learn from mindful practices by asking them to reflect. What did you notice? Did your mind wander? Did you feel your breathing change?

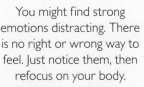

You might find strong emotions distracting. There is no right or wrong way to feel. Just notice them, then refocus on your body.

Notice how your breath matches your feelings, such as sleepy or awake.

If you are worrying, it might change your breathing. Just notice.

The left side of the heart beats stronger than the right, so you might feel it more easily if you place your hand slightly to the left of the centre of your chest.

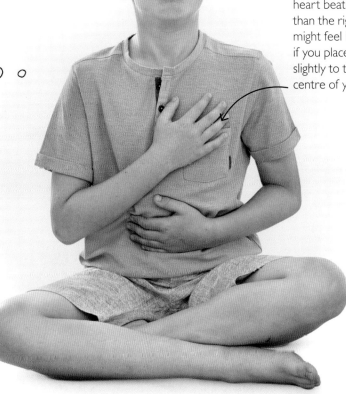

Check in on you

Place one hand over your heart and the other on your belly. Feel your breath moving and maybe your heart beating. Thoughts and emotions might pop into your mind. Simply notice them and refocus on your body.

Gratitude paper chain

Time can seem to go very fast and we forget the little things that make us happy. This activity can help you be mindful of all the things that you are grateful for.

FOR THE GROWN-UPS...

You can help your child think about what they are grateful for by asking questions. What are you really good at and enjoy doing? What makes you smile?

What you'll need:

- Different-coloured pieces of paper
- Safety scissors
- A pen
- A glue stick or sticky tape

1. **Cut some strips of coloured paper** using safety scissors. They need to be wide enough to write on.

2 **Write something you are grateful for** on each strip. Think about what makes you smile.

My friends

3 **Make a ring** with the first strip, using glue or tape to stick the ends together. Then thread another strip through the first to make a second ring. Keep going to make a chain.

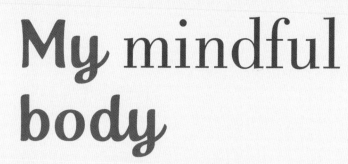

My mindful body

Mindfulness means paying attention without judgement, but with care. Spend five minutes noticing the different parts of your body. Try not to think about whether you like them, but of how useful they are!

Notice your feet. Your toes might feel warm or cool. Move your attention along your foot, to the arch and then the heel.

Move your attention to your breath as it enters your lungs. Is it harder or easier to notice the inside of your body?

Shift your focus to your legs. Think about how much you use them for walking, running, and jumping! Send them some warm appreciation for all that they do.

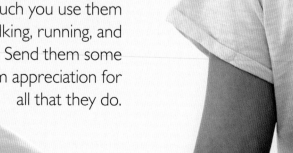

☀ FOR THE GROWN-UPS...

Noticing each part of the body without judgement can be a first step to feeling positive about your body. Encourage your child to think about each bit without criticism.

5

Focus attention on your arms. Are they heavy or light? Move your focus along your arms from the tips of your fingers to your shoulders.

4

Notice any soft or tense muscles in your face. Explore your forehead, eyes, nose, ears, and mouth with your attention.

Notice how each part feels, and remember not to judge them.

6

Can you feel the strength in your arm? Does it feel the same if your arm is bent?

My **mindful** plan

For mindfulness to be helpful, you need to practise it regularly. Try making a mindful plan for yourself. See where you can fit in a few mindful minutes each day.

Try to check in on how you are feeling throughout the day. It might help you remember if you do it at certain times each day, such as when you wake up, at lunchtime, and before you go to bed. Why not try a mindful practice, too?

1) Wake up, check in. How do you feel right now? What emotions are you feeling? Focus on your body. You might try the feet, seat, and hands practice on page 14.

2) Lunchtime reset. You might be feeling ready for a change by the middle of the day. Try a yawn to reset on page 46 or a rainbow breath on page 32 to raise your energy for the afternoon.

3) Ready for sleep. You might need to calm down before bedtime. Try the high-five breath on page 21 and focus on your breathing.

Aim to have a mindful goal of the day. It can be as small as stopping to focus on what you are feeling for one minute.

Today I will...

You can plan ahead so you have a mindful activity ready for when you need it. It doesn't have to be as big as the crafts in this book. You could simply sketch a pattern to colour in later.

Be creative with mindful colouring. Draw shapes, then fill them in as you like. Enjoy the colours and shapes – it doesn't have to be perfect.

At the end of the day, reflect on what went well. Were you able to try something mindful? What did you see that you might not have noticed if you weren't being mindful?

I spotted a feather in the park.

It was small, and it was white at

one end and brown at the other.

Restful routine

Sleep isn't always easy. In fact it can be very hard to fall asleep and even harder to get back to sleep if you wake up in the night. You can learn how to prepare yourself for sleep using a restful routine.

Set-up for sleep

Relax before you go to bed and try to get up at the same time every day.

Make sure your room is:
• Tidy
• Quiet
• Dark (a night light is okay)
• A comfortable temperature

Why do we sleep?

Our bodies use the time we are asleep to grow, repair, and reset for a new day. When we don't sleep, we get tired and unhappy.

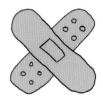

Healing
Sleep gives your body time to repair itself. It's a time when your muscles can rest, heal, and get stronger.

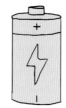

Energy
Without sleep you get tired very quickly. Sleep re-energizes your brain, ready to learn new things.

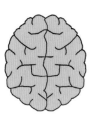

Memory
Your brain uses the time when you are asleep to sort through new memories and to store important ones.

Growth
You grow most when you are asleep. During the night, your body releases a chemical that makes you grow.

Give yourself time to relax before you go to bed.

Bright and blue light

Bright lights can make it hard for your brain to slow down and sleep. Blue light in particular tells your brain that it is daytime. Electronic devices can give off blue light. Try turning off any screens an hour before you go to bed to help make you feel sleepy.

Avoid electronic devices before bedtime.

You should be getting around 10-12 hours of sleep a night.

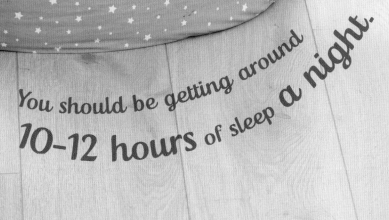

Try this

Make a bedtime chart with steps to follow to help prepare you for sleep. Grouping the tasks in pairs can be helpful.

- Change your clothes and brush your teeth.
- Do a calming mindful practice and get into bed.
- Turn the lights down and close your eyes.

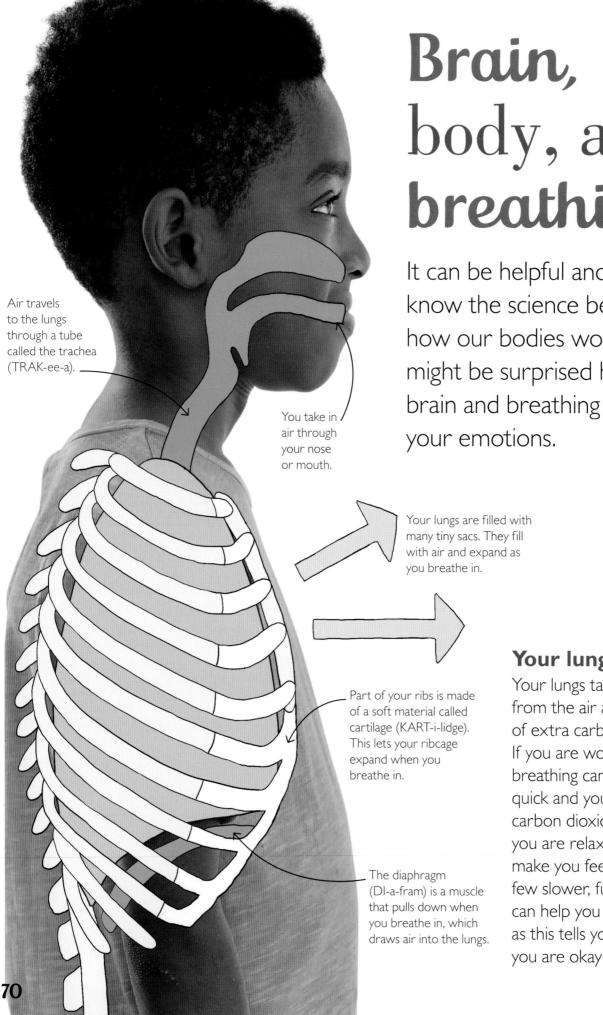

Brain, body, and breathing

It can be helpful and fun to know the science behind how our bodies work. You might be surprised how your brain and breathing affect your emotions.

Air travels to the lungs through a tube called the trachea (TRAK-ee-a).

You take in air through your nose or mouth.

Your lungs are filled with many tiny sacs. They fill with air and expand as you breathe in.

Part of your ribs is made of a soft material called cartilage (KART-i-lidge). This lets your ribcage expand when you breathe in.

The diaphragm (DI-a-fram) is a muscle that pulls down when you breathe in, which draws air into the lungs.

Your lungs

Your lungs take in oxygen from the air and get rid of extra carbon dioxide. If you are worried, your breathing can become quick and you lose more carbon dioxide than when you are relaxed, which can make you feel anxious. A few slower, fuller breaths can help you feel calmer, as this tells your brain that you are okay and safe.

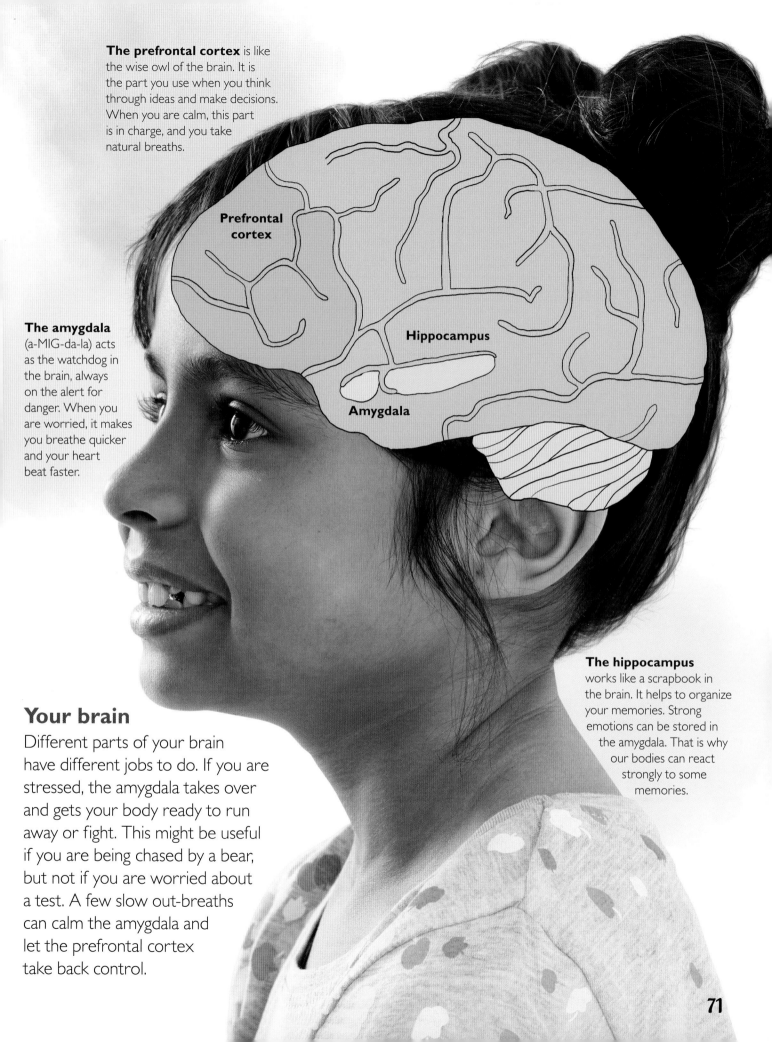

The prefrontal cortex is like the wise owl of the brain. It is the part you use when you think through ideas and make decisions. When you are calm, this part is in charge, and you take natural breaths.

Prefrontal cortex

Hippocampus

Amygdala

The amygdala (a-MIG-da-la) acts as the watchdog in the brain, always on the alert for danger. When you are worried, it makes you breathe quicker and your heart beat faster.

The hippocampus works like a scrapbook in the brain. It helps to organize your memories. Strong emotions can be stored in the amygdala. That is why our bodies can react strongly to some memories.

Your brain

Different parts of your brain have different jobs to do. If you are stressed, the amygdala takes over and gets your body ready to run away or fight. This might be useful if you are being chased by a bear, but not if you are worried about a test. A few slow out-breaths can calm the amygdala and let the prefrontal cortex take back control.

71

Index

Acknowledgements

DK would like to thank the following: The models; model agencies Zebedee Management and Urban Angels; Juliana Sergot for hair and make-up; Romi Chakraborty for design help; Katy Lennon for editorial help; Caroline Hunt for proofreading; Helen Peters for indexing; Sakshi Saluja for picture research.

The publisher would like to thank the following for their kind permission to reproduce their photographs:
(Key: a-above; b-below/bottom; c-centre; f-far; l-left; r-right; t-top) **5** Taylor Brown Photography: (cr). **18-19** 123RF.com: linux87. **28-29** Dreamstime.com: Lunamarina. **40-41** Getty Images: Andriy Prokopenko. **50-51** Getty Images: Mitch Diamond. **54** 123RF.com: PaylessImages (tl). **Dreamstime.com:** Andor Bujdoso (br). **55** 123RF.com: Leszek Czerwonka (cl). **Dreamstime.com:** Rusel1981 (tl)

All other images © Dorling Kindersley
For further information see: www.dkimages.com